The Firehouse Light

BY *Janet Nolan*   ILLUSTRATED BY *Marie Lafrance*

TRICYCLE PRESS
Berkeley

A long time ago, when horse-drawn buggies delivered ice to keep food cold, and laundry dried on ropes in the sun, fires were fought with buckets, axes, and hand-pulled carts with water hoses.

In one little town on a moonless night, a cry rang out: "Fire!"

Out of bed the townspeople leapt. As they lined up in bucket brigades, they lent their voices to the rising cry.

"Get the hose cart!"

"Grab the buckets!"

Volunteer firefighters ran through the night toward the wooden shack where the firefighting equipment was kept. They threw open the doors, but it was dark inside and hard to see.

"Light a lantern!" one man yelled.

"Hold it high!" called another as they reached inside the pitch-black shack, wheeled out the hose cart, and raced to put out the fire.

Finding firefighting equipment in the dark was not easy.

Then one day a businessman gave the firefighters a gift. No longer would they have to waste time lighting lanterns. A wire burning inside a ball of glass would light the way.

Day after day, year after year, the lightbulb did not burn out.

After **TEN YEARS**, the wooden shack was gone but the lightbulb was not. In a firehouse with walls and windows, the four-watt lightbulb was never turned off. A soft orange light, it glowed no brighter than a handful of fireflies.

Beneath the lightbulb, firefighters polished the hose cart until it shined. They would be marching in the little town's Fourth of July parade.

Flags waved. A band played. Dogs barked and children cheered as they marched on newly paved roads past businesses and homes recently wired with electricity.

And along with the clopping of horses' hooves a new sound was heard: the loud, squeaky honk of a car's horn.

Day after day, year after year, the lightbulb did not burn out.

After TWENTY YEARS, the lightbulb was no longer the brightest in the firehouse. Other bulbs shined brighter during the day, and in the evening, after the sun had set, they illuminated the night. But to the firefighters the four-watt bulb was the most important. It burned when they left to fight a fire and was still lit when they returned.

No longer was news of a fire spread by cries and shouts. When a fire broke out, townspeople could call the telephone switchboard operator.

Volunteer firefighters, who lived in their own homes and worked at separate jobs, heard the town's fire bell ring and knew it was time to stop working on farms, in fields, in offices and shops. Off they went, not pulling a hose cart but driving a brand-new fire engine with a bell on top.

Day after day, year after year, the lightbulb did not burn out.

After **THIRTY YEARS**, cars were driven up and down the streets of the little town.

"Careful. Look both ways," firefighters reminded children running to the theater, where they would watch movies on the big picture screen for twenty-five cents apiece.

In the firehouse, a record spun on the record player as firefighters cleaned and inspected the hoses and the gauges, the wheels and the windshields. They checked their boots, their smoke masks, and the tools they carried on their wide belts. Firefighters never knew when a fire would break out, so they needed to be ready.

Day after day, year after year, the lightbulb did not burn out.

After FORTY YEARS, trains rumbled into the newly built station, airplanes flew overhead, and firefighters gathered around the radio to hear the day's news. All of a sudden the siren blared.

Beneath a lightbulb that glowed strong and steady, firefighters stepped into their big boots, pulled on their heavy coats, put thick helmets on their heads, and switched on their two-way radios.

They drove through the growing town's only traffic signal, honking the horn. Instead of fire or smoke, they found a crowd gathered near a tree, pointing at a boy who had climbed too high and couldn't get down.

Day after day, year after year, the lightbulb did not burn out.

After FIFTY YEARS, the little town was not so little anymore. Families moved into brand-new homes and parked their cars in the driveway. And all over town, workers were busy building new schools, hospitals, highways, libraries, and ice cream shops.

Firefighters were no longer volunteers. They were paid employees who lived and worked in the firehouse.

A refrigerator kept their food cold and a stove heated it up. They vacuumed with a vacuum cleaner, watched television on a black-and-white TV, and at night they slept beneath the glow of the four-watt bulb.

Day after day, year after year, the lightbulb did not burn out.

After more than SIXTY YEARS, on television sets across the big town, everyone watched something they had never seen before: a man walking on the moon.

Twenty-four hours a day, seven days a week, the lightbulb burned strong and steady above the heads of firefighters who practiced, trained, and were always prepared.

Day after day, year after year—for ten, twenty, thirty, forty, fifty, sixty, SEVENTY YEARS—the lightbulb glowed. But in 1976, it stopped.

The firefighters were moving to a new firehouse, but not without their lightbulb. The lightbulb, the socket, the cord, and the porcelain outlet that attached it to the ceiling were carefully removed.

Fire engine lights flashed and sirens blared. Flags waved. A band played. Dogs barked and children cheered as the lightbulb, the star of the town's parade, was driven to its new home.

All eyes were on the electrician as he reconnected the lightbulb. Would it light? Would it still glow? A second passed and then another. The bulb did not light. The people held their breath. The lightbulb still did not light. The electrician jiggled the switch, and then the bulb, as it always had, flickered and started to glow.

Day after day, year after year, the lightbulb did not burn out.

After EIGHTY YEARS, the lightbulb stood guard over the fire engines from fifteen feet above. Schoolchildren came to the firehouse to learn about fire safety. The men and women who worked as firefighters explained how they raise the ladder on the hook and ladder truck, how they breathe through oxygen masks, and why they wear fire-retardant uniforms.

Beneath the glow of a four-watt bulb they taught children to *stop, drop,* and *roll.*

Day after day, year after year, the lightbulb did not burn out.

NINETY YEARS after the cries of townspeople alerted firefighters and a lightbulb helped them find their equipment in the dark, a 911 call could be made and computers would pinpoint the exact location of the emergency call.

With sirens blaring and red lights flashing, firefighters, paramedics, and police cars raced down the crowded streets of the city. They raced past halogen, fluorescent, and incandescent lights, past neon and strobe lights, traffic lights and streetlights, motorcycle, car, truck, and bus lights. Driving though the night, help was on the way.

Day after day, year after year, the lightbulb did not burn out.

After **ONE HUNDRED YEARS** it was time for a birthday party! The town turned out to celebrate. Television and radio crews set up their gear. Speeches were made, pictures taken, birthday cake eaten, and "Happy Birthday" sung to a one-hundred-year-old lightbulb that had never once burned out.

Strong and steady, it still glows
above the heads of firefighters —
it burns when they leave to fight a fire
and stays lit after they return.

Afterword

IN 1901 MR. DENNIS BERNAL, owner of the Livermore Power and Light Company, gave the volunteer firefighters of Livermore, California, a four-watt lightbulb made of carbon filament and hand-blown glass. The lightbulb was manufactured by the Shelby Electric Company of Shelby, Ohio, and was placed above the town's firefighting equipment, where it helped firefighters see in the dark. It has been burning ever since.

No one knows for sure why the lightbulb has lasted so long. It might be because the bulb has hardly ever been turned off or it might be the lack of wear and tear. Today the lightbulb hangs from a single cord twenty feet above the ground in the Livermore-Pleasanton Fire Department's Station #6. The lightbulb has its own backup generator to protect it during power outages, and its own webcam and Web site: www.centennialbulb.org.

For more than one hundred years of American history, through tragedies and triumphs, the firehouse light has glowed.

PHOTOGRAPH: DICK JONES

Thanks to Tom and Megan for the light they bring to my life.
—J. N.

To my daughter, Béatrice, for her constant help and encouragement.
—M. L.

J 363.370
15.99
Amazon
9/10

a true
story! :)

Text copyright © 2010 by Janet Nolan
Illustrations copyright © 2010 by Marie Lafrance

All rights reserved.
Published in the United States by Tricycle Press,
an imprint of the Crown Publishing Group,
a division of Random House, Inc., New York.
www.crownpublishing.com
www.tricyclepress.com

Tricycle Press and the Tricycle Press colophon are
registered trademarks of Random House, Inc.

Library of Congress Cataloging-in-Publication Data
Nolan, Janet.
The firehouse light / by Janet Nolan ; illustrations
by Marie Lafrance.
   p. cm.
1. Fire stations — California — Livermore —
History— Juvenile literature. 2. Fire extinction
— California — Livermore — History — Juvenile
literature. 3. Fire safety — California — Livermore
— History — Juvenile literature. 4. Incandescent
lamps — California — Livermore — History —
Juvenile literature. I. Lafrance, Marie, ill. II. Title.
TH9148.N65 2010
363.3709794'65—dc22   2009007964

ISBN 978-1-58246-298-1 (hardcover)
ISBN 978-1-58246-346-9 (Gibraltar lib. bdg.)

Printed in China
Design by Lisa Diercks
Typeset in Archer
The illustrations were rendered
in acrylics.

1 2 3 4 5 6 — 14 13 12 11 10

First Edition